Enduring Health:
Profound Simplicity

Enduring Health: Profound Simplicity

Michael Hewitt MD

ISBN 978-0-615-72316-7

Author's Note

We have these truly amazing bodies, capable of so much. The process of walking around our local lake or climbing Mount Everest is a scientific marvel. Our muscles, bones, nerves, blood vessels and brain make the most complicated entity in the universe. As I went through school, learning the complexity of the human body constantly left me in awe. This fantastic body is ours for only a short time. I have been fortunate to enjoy running. Through years of racing, my admiration has continued to grow for one particular participant, the atypical runner. Watching the self described "non-runner" jog, walk and crawl to the finish line and their subsequent elation almost brings me to tears. Most do it for one reason, to see what they are capable of, and I find this wonderful! The accomplishment of hiking the local hill or walking in a charity race with friends can be profound. The act of walking around the block after dinner as a family, talking about the day in the fresh air, tightens bonds. Exercise does not have to mean fancy shoes and a gym, it simply means to move. It comes in endless forms, from raking leaves to walking the dog to running a marathon and everything in between.

This book was not made as a joke or novelty. It comes from a profound concern regarding our population's well-being. As a practicing orthopedic surgeon in one of the fittest states in the U.S., I am disheartened by the deterioration of our health.

We are inundated on a daily basis with new techniques which promise weight loss. The problem lies in the fact that most diet fads fail. Eliminating a food group may decrease caloric intake for a while, but the habit is not sustainable. In no shape or form is weight loss a guarantee of health. Quite the opposite, too low of a body weight can be as unhealthy as obesity. Food, with its energy and nutrients, fuels our bodies. In addition, most find great pleasure in eating. Eating less does not mean eliminating one food group, it means consuming less of all food. Our bodies are programmed to save excess calories for a time of need. For most of us, this time of need never comes and the excess calories become excess pounds. As the pounds accumulate, they alter how our bodies work. They affect our joints, heart, blood vessels, breathing, blood pressure and sugars, to name just a few. They affect our ability to perform even the most simple of tasks and limit our ability to directly experience the world around us.

What I am proposing is far from novel. Describing the words in this book as an oversimplification is an understatement. As I toyed with the idea in my head, I kept adding words or chapters, thinking more information would add to the theme. I then realized in such a muddled topic, less was more. Much more. That the only real way to be a healthier weight was to "eat less, move more" struck me as profound, even empowering. Do we all have to run marathons and eat salad for every meal? Of coarse not. Mom's advice, "everything in moderation", rings true. The change in habit does not have to be drastic. Maintaining weight by addressing both input and output increases the chance for success. Having a body that can walk in the park, through the mall or to a friend's house enhances our life. Too many people have become prisoners in their own body, unable to accomplish even the most simple of adventures as a result of obesity. I find that a shame.

Simple does not mean easy. I write this with optimism and the humble goal to spark a conversation and simplify the confusing topic of health. The most meaningful entry of this book is yours, chapter 3. Providing pictures of smiling faces in motion, enjoying these brilliant bodies, realizes the purpose of this book, and in doing so, hopefully makes your time on this wondrous earth more fulfilling.

Support is crucial. The ideas, drawings and pictures in this book were a family endeavor. I propose we make the family evening walk a new national tradition, getting people off the couch and spending time moving together. Enduring health, profoundly simple.

Enjoying views of his
childhood, 60 years later

Never entered a gym or
a race but ALWAYS
moving, even at 97!

Superman flying

Kids chasing a
sunrise, nothing better

Chapter 1

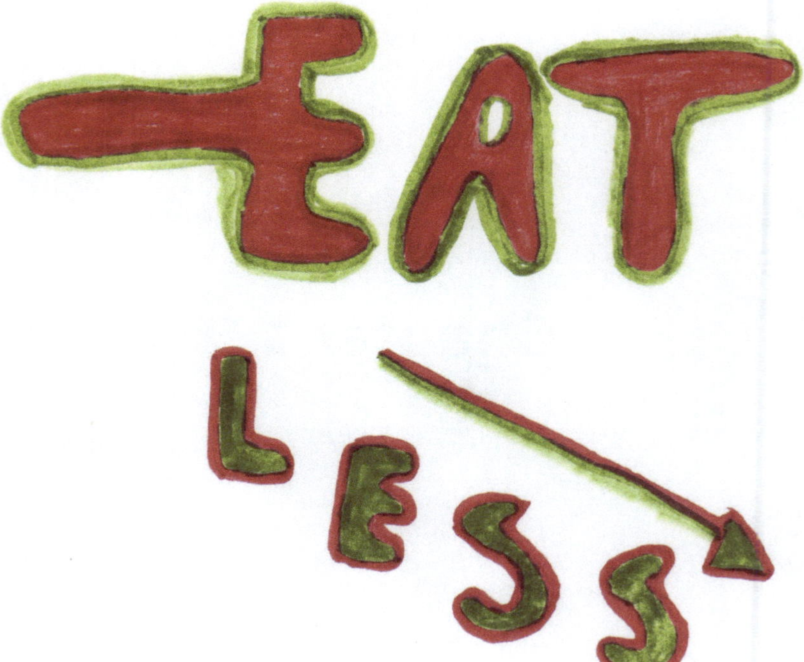
EAT
LESS

Chapter 2

Chapter 3